My Little Soldier

A Graduate from the Totally Traumatic Toddler Academy

Tammy Kovar

ISBN 979-8-89243-371-6 (paperback)
ISBN 979-8-88943-587-7 (hardcover)
ISBN 979-8-88943-586-0 (digital)

Christian Faith Publishing
832 Park Avenue
Meadville, PA 16335
www.christianfaithpublishing.com

Printed in the United States of America

To my hubby Kenny, my son Dion, and my daughter Kala for being who you are…*amazing*! I love you and am *so proud* of all of you! (And yes, I'm showing my "blue" for everyone to see!) And special recognition goes to Kala for without her, this book would not be a reality. May you never stop making others laugh!

To my mom Iris and my aunt Betty for listening to me as I have talked incessantly about this writing journey with them. And to Brenda, my soul sister, for her support and wisdom.

To Abba Father for blessing me with the passion for writing and for my corner of the world filled with precious family and friends! I am so humbly thankful!

I was at war! A full-fledged war to maintain control of my sanity and my somewhat-composed being. For you see, I had a toddler; an active, over-inquisitive toddler. This eighteen-month-old was staging battles to put me into the land of the "burned-out," "stressed-out," and "pooped-out."

This girl spent her nine months in the womb not only getting all those tiny parts in the right place but also plotting and scheming to win a war with her momma. For you see, she was a graduate from the Totally Traumatic Toddler Academy and majored in "Making Mom a Mess." And after reading of her antics, I believe you will agree with me that she graduated at the top of her class.

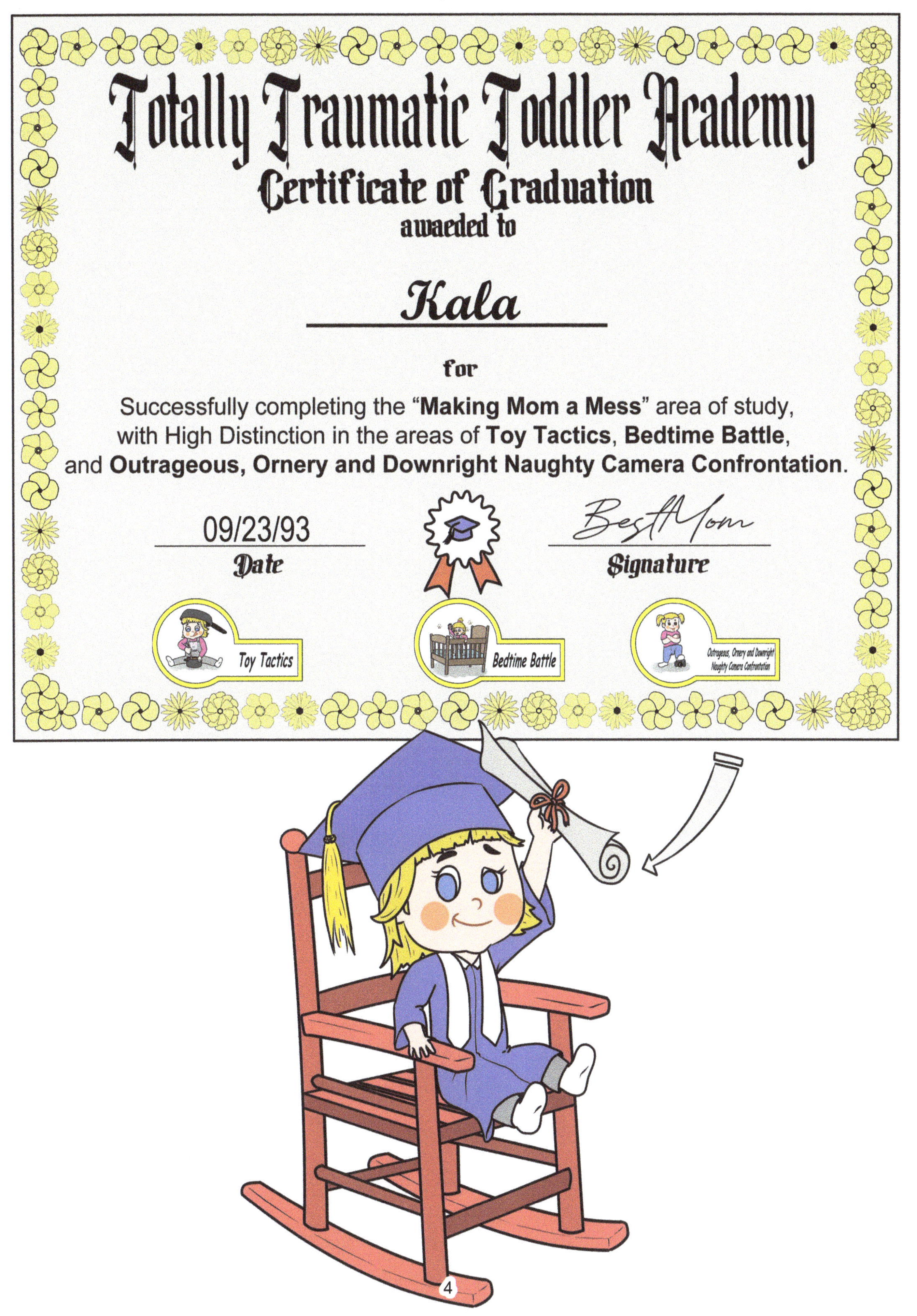

Totally Traumatic Toddler Academy
Certificate of Graduation
awaeded to

Kala

for

Successfully completing the "Making Mom a Mess" area of study,
with High Distinction in the areas of Toy Tactics, Bedtime Battle,
and Outrageous, Ornery and Downright Naughty Camera Confrontation.

09/23/93
Date

Best Mom
Signature

Toy Tactics
Bedtime Battle
Outrageous, Ornery and Downright Naughty Camera Confrontation

4

Toy Tactics

Bedtime Battle

Outrageous, Ornery and Downright Naughty Camera Confrontation

Three of our most intense confrontations were the "toy tactics," the "bedtime battle," and the "outrageous, ornery, and downright naughty camera confrontation."

The "toy tactics" maneuver was an ongoing struggle with all the chew toys, stuffed animals, and things considered "toys for toddlers." The first rule was: *Don't play with them*. Instead, it is much more infuriating for Mom to perform the "mouth Inspection test," shoving things in her mouth I needed a microscope to see. It was also more energy sapping for Mom if she pulled out all the pans, bowls, and anything in the lower cupboards within reach (like the flour and oil—why, oh why, hadn't I moved those) and played with those, not the toys. Definitely *not* the toys!

"DON'T PLAY WITH THEM!"

Another maneuver within the "toy tactics" strategy has become known as the "million mile trail." It explained why we had dishes in the bathroom and toilet paper in the kitchen. Let me give you an example (and you can follow her journey on the following pages). It started simply enough when she threw the garbage from the bathroom into the tub. Then she grabbed the toilet paper and darted to the kitchen. There she promptly exchanged the toilet paper for a pot from the cupboard. From there, she headed back to the bathroom, depositing the pot. Then it was on to the dining room where she dropped the magazines she had picked up from the bathroom. At this point, she turned her focus to an unbreakable knickknack (I learned the first day her feet hit the floor the breakables had to go).

When she scampered into the living room, the knickknack was discarded, and she went for the ultimate challenge, Dad's TV remote. Oh, the times our household came to a complete standstill until that controller was found. Everyone stopped what they were doing, and the hunt was on. Her best battle move was to throw the remote in the dirty clothes basket. We didn't find it for days.

This little maneuver was extremely frustrating for her daddy. This room-to-room sabotage took only five minutes to create, but it took me a couple of hours to pick up. And when her nap was over, it started all over again. Ah, yes, the joys of toddlerhood.

MILLION
START HERE
Toy Tactics
11

ILE TRAIL

The second and most ingenious strategy my blond-haired daughter contrived has become known as the "bedtime battle." The first maneuver was the sheet sham. She was probably the only toddler who preferred to sleep without sheets. She could not close those beautiful blue eyes until the sheets were completely ripped off her bed and thrown to the floor. I actually put the sheets back on her bed three times in one night only to find her the next morning once again sleeping on a bare, cool mattress. Well, with a little creativity, I won this particular battle. I wrapped a full-size sheet around her mattress twice. Problem solved.

Bedtime Battle

FINGER PAINTING

15

But was the "bedtime battle" over? Certainly not. She had more artillery. We've notoriously named it "finger painting." Now that she couldn't strip her bed, she turned her attention to her clothes. Simply said, they came off, even the diaper. Unfortunately, unveiling the diaper revealed another surprise, for she had just had a "movement." She let the artist in her bubble to the surface, using anything within reach for her "artwork." After a late-night bath, washing the sheets, and scrubbing the wall and her crib with disinfectant, I knew I needed to quickly counter a defense because I wasn't doing this twice in the wee hours of the night. I mobilized my new arsenal attack. Baby pins! Yes, baby pins. I promptly put those pins in her fresh new diaper on her baby-powder-scented body and firmly attached, ensuring they were toddler proof. This was a proud moment for Mom! I'd won this one!

But my toddler wasn't about to stop there. She moved right on to the "outrageous, ornery, and downright naughty, camera confrontation." It all began when I made the decision to take her toddler pictures myself instead of expensive studio pictures. I planned and planned and then planned more, spending weeks preparing the perfect outfit to go with a creative backdrop and the appropriate props. I had a red taffeta dress with a white bow for her hair, white tights with precious black leather shoes to be set against an all-white backdrop. Her red rocker and all her favorite toys and stuffed animals would grace the portrait with just enough contrast and color to create that perfect photo. The second outfit was a bright, fun, and colorful romper that brought out her eyes and screamed adorable (good thing photos usually don't portray ornery). For this photo shoot, I was planning on using a blue backdrop. And of course, no portrait session is complete without the old-fashioned washtub full of nose tickling bubbles. The rubber duck, shower cap, and scrubber were on hand as well. These shots would use the "natural" look.

Outrageous, Ornery and Downright
Naughty Camera Confrontation

18

Outrageous, Ornery and Downright
Naughty Camera Confrontation

Oh, I was all set. It was Saturday morning, and everything was in place. I was beaming with pride at the money I was saving and the creativity I was using pulling together the perfect outfits, backdrops and props. I was anxious to try my hand at photography (a hobby I always wanted to pursue).

And then it happened! The bathroom door was left open (don't ever do this with an active and inquisitive toddler, not if you value your possessions and your toddler. Besides, it cuts the million mile trail down to 750,000). My precious little academy graduate found my camera. She obviously passed the obstacle course drill with flying colors as she was able to navigate onto the kitchen table and proceed to climb down successfully, all without being detected. She scampered into the bathroom and proceeded to destroy the only instrument that could make the pictures reality, my camera!

Outrageous, Ornery and Downright
Naughty Camera Confrontation

Outrageous, Ornery and Downright
Naughty Camera Confrontation

When I heard an unexplained and unusual sound, I ran to investigate. She had thrown my camera into the toilet! Yes, the toilet! Exasperated, I picked my camera out of the toilet with water running out of every little nook, screw, and crack. She'd won. There would be no pictures today. And instead of saving myself some money, it was going to cost me double (a new camera and studio pictures). This battle was my most bitter defeat.

These interactions were quite taxing on this momma. I often had to refill my artillery—patience, energy, and composure during her quiet times (a.k.a., when she was sleeping).

As time went on, the skirmishes lessened after the camera incident. I think she felt she had accomplished her goal and represented her training well. She had succeeded.

"THANK YOU EVER SO MUCH, LORD, FOR MY LITTLE SOLDIER"

And the best part of these little battles were the end of the day as I tucked her in bed, fluffing her blankets lightly around her face, kissing her gently on her forehead, and muttering, "I'm tucking you in the way my mom tucked me in, so hold on to this tuck as long as you can." And before I turned off the lights and closed the door, I turned and looked at my lovely, quiet toddler and thought, *Thank you ever so much, Lord, for my little soldier*, as I wiped the wetness from my eyes.

My toddler eventually outgrew her academy training
and into a beautiful, intelligent adult and one of my
closest friends. Now, we both look back on these sweet
memories with laughter that warm our hearts.
So to all you moms with a precious little one who has also
graduated from the Totally Traumatic Toddler Academy,
take heart. You will win some and lose some, but the
beauty is in the battle itself. And I'm pulling for you!

MY LITTLE SOLDIER
Her Antics
By: Tommy K. Kovar

About the Author

Tammy and her daughter, the inspiring "Little Soldier"

Tammy Kovar is a mom who has braved the toddler battleground. When the tantics of her second-born brought to the surface the stressful moments of mothering, Tammy turned to journaling, a passion since high school. She often uses this tool to work through life's issues, capture daily events, and write ramblings on various topics.

Most of Tammy's life was spent working and supporting her family in their many passions, so there was little time for writing. But upon retiring, she dusted off the *My Little Soldier* manuscript and, at the urging of several family members, submitted it for publication. Her daughter (the main character of this story) is now a beautiful, full-of-life young woman that brings laughter and happiness with her wherever she goes.

Tammy lives in a small Nebraska town and is enjoying retirement immensely by spending time with her hubby of thirty-six years, her adult children, her first grandchild, and her close circle of family and friends.

You can read more about Tammy at tammykovar.org where she has several journaling templates, including one for moms who want to journal their own battle stories.